VOLUME I

The Sacred Gates

13 Original Rabbinic Parables
To Enter The Palace Of Wisdom

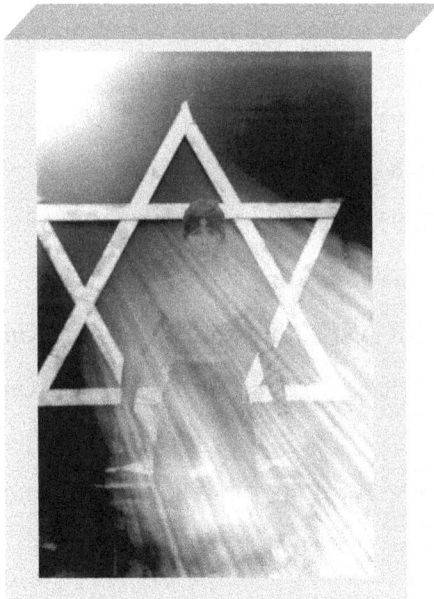

Child-Time Publishers

Established 1988

www.childtimepublishers.com

Library of Congress Number: 9780929934051

First Edition: January 2018

ISBN: 978-0-929934-05-1 (softcover)

Cover Art: Arlene Kingston

Logo Design: Sabina K. Mintz & Eric Sander Kingston

Photos Of Eric Sander Kingston By: William Kingston

Printed In USA

W.o.W.

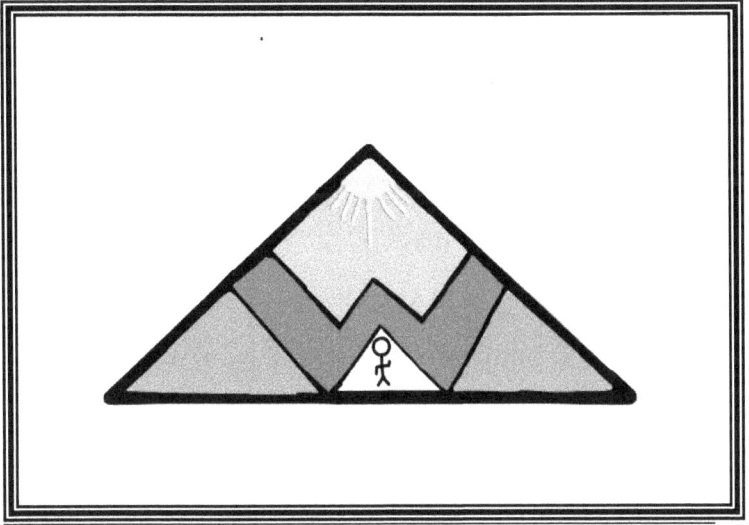

Wish On Wisdom ™

There was once a person, who was granted from Heaven, a wish. They could either wish for wealth, or wish for wisdom. The person replied: "I wish for wisdom. For through wisdom, I will attain great wealth."

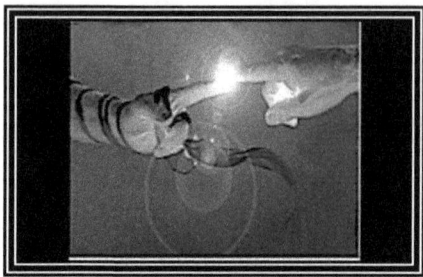

How To Use This Book

10 Power Prayer Of Divine Protection

1. May you surpass your teachers

2. May you go beyond yourself

3. May you leave a legacy of truth, love and justice

4. May you be an example of dignity

5. May your powers be used to unite all people, "not serve the vanity" of a single person

6. May you always be grateful for the smallest of things

7. May you never say "yes" when you mean "no"

8. May all your past hurts become the lessons that guide you towards your constructive destiny

9. May you see the greatest strength is within, when it connects constructively to others

And most of all

10. May you see, "The pain you feel is from the love you withhold."

Table Of Contents

Yelling In The Dark?...........................6

Yelling In The Dark Again?...................8

What Makes A Faithful King..................10

We All Need Something........................12

The Department Store Temple................14

In A Different Way..............................16

The Power Of Choice..........................18

Impossible Faith...............................20

The Custodian And The Angels.............22

The True Success Of Failure.................24

The Ink Of The Story..........................26

A Flood Of Tears...............................28

The Beauty Of The King.....................30

Acknowledgments 32

About Eric.....................................34

Further Information...........................36

Other Books By Child Time Publishers.....37

Yelling In The Dark

Part I

A man was asked by the Head Rabbi to go to the back room of the temple to find a book about the value of patience. The man got up from his place of study and went. As he entered the back room he could not find the light switch. He instantly became frustrated. Suddenly, he bumped square into someone with a hat and jacket on. "Fool!" cried the man, "Can't you be more mindful! If you too could not find the light switch, why did you not alert me you were in the room? Don't you have any common sense!!!" Suddenly, the light went on, and the man saw he was standing in front of the Rabbi's jacket and hat, that were hanging on the wall. Entering the room, the shocked Rabbi just asked, "Who on earth are you yelling at?"

Insight: When we lose our temper before we understand what is going on, we lose sight of reality, and the fool we are yelling at, is our own impatience.

Question: Where in your life is impatience interfering with you?

Agreement: I, _____, agree and commit to, for myself, to choosing patience over anger when my circumstances seem to be not in my control.

Yelling In The Dark

part II

The Rabbi asked a man in the temple to go to the back room to get him a book on the awareness of the mind. The man got up from his place of study and went. As he entered the back room, he could not find the light switch and became frustrated again. He then, clearly saw someone standing in front of him. So, he asked for assistance with finding the light switch. The man did not answer. "Idiot!" said the man "I see you right before me! Can you not even answer me! Have you no respect for your fellow!" Suddenly, the light went on, and he saw he was standing in front of a mirror. As the Rabbi entered the room, he asked him (again) "Who on earth are you yelling at now?"

Insight: Assuming is not awareness and often leads one not only to looking like a fool to others, but seeing a fool in the mirror as well.

Question: Where in my life am I acting before I get all the facts?

Agreement: I,_____, agree and commit to, for myself, to gathering correct information BEFORE going into action.

What Makes A Faithful King

A young Rabbi went to the senior Rabbi and said, "King Solomon was very wise. Yet, his personal choices caused him much suffering and regret. At the end of his days, King Solomon must have sensed the error of his personal ways and wondered "Why?" He must have called out to G-d for an answer to his "why?" Yet, all he got was silence and felt "ignored" in a way. Did G-d ignore King Solomon at the end?" The senior Rabbi thought for a moment and said, "Well, when you come right down to it, what would or could G-d say to King Solomon? King Solomon had great Wisdom, vast Knowledge. He had the right Father, King David. He built the Temple with his power and intellect. I believe, the silence was not G-d ignoring him. I believe the silence WAS G-d's Answer to King Solomon. The silence meant, "You are the one with vast wisdom, and writings and inheritance. What more should I add to the great wealth you already possess? At this level, even I have to allow you your freewill to choose, because ONLY THEN will I, the I Am, see if you are a true and faithful king on all levels. ONLY THEN, Solomon, will I be able to see if all your vast wisdom applies, not only to the world, but more importantly, to your own life as well."

The Insight: Make sure you are ruler over your OWN internal kingdom.

The Question: Where in your life could you be more aligned with your own teaching and words?

Agreement: I,_____, agree and commit to, for myself, to aligning my thoughts, speech and action.

We All Need Something

Individuality Vs. Isolation

The head Rabbi, had a student who was always apart from the other students. He always sought to do everything on his own. One day, the head Rabbi spoke with the student about this, and asked him why he refused to really work with others. "I don't want to be like everyone else and I don't require anything." The head Rabbi said, "G-d didn't create you to be like anyone else, but you. But G-d, didn't create the things in this world, and people in it, to be like islands. G-d Created things and people to eventually work together. Just consider, that Abraham needed even the idols to show G-d his belief. Queen Ester, needed the king to assist the Jewish People. King David, needed his slingshot. Moses needed the Burning Bush, Aaron, his Staff and the Ark. G-d could of freed the slaves Himself, and done All things Himself, but EVEN G-d choose to use others. What makes you so special?"

Insight: Many people who choose to be "islands" end up alone.

Question: Where in your life can you be more interactive with friends and workers?

Agreement: I,_____, commit and agree to, for myself, to understanding that I do not lose my individuality by being part of a team.

The Department Store Temple

One day, a Rabbi had a vision to construct a magnificent temple for the community. He spent many years designing, and then building this Divine Structure. Every time someone asked the Rabbi when it would be done, he said, "Someday soon." Finally, the temple was complete, but the Rabbi did not want anyone to enter, for the temple, to him, was a perfect blessing and gift. "If I let people in, surely things would get dirtied, messed up and broken!" People yearned to come, for a while, but then went to other temple's not as nice, but in use. After a few years, the Rabbi seemed to just disappear. The new owners of the Rabbi's building had no interest in a temple. They simply removed the books and converted it into a department store. The people entering the department store all commented on how beautiful and perfect the store was, filled with a plethora of items and shiny gifts all, very appealing to the eyes, but of which had little value to the Soul.

Insight: G-d puts thing's here on earth for their Light to be used, not to be or remain perfect.

Question: Where in your life are your gifts not being put to use and hidden away?

Agreement: I, _____ agree and commit to, for myself, to share the light, wisdom and gifts that I have already attained.

In A Different Way

When the Alter Rebbe was released from prison, many celebrated at the release from his confinement. One such person, upon seeing the Alter Rebbe, approached and asked him, "Dear Rebbe, how does it feel to be out of your prison and your confinement?" The Alter Rebbe looked at the man and said, "My Prison and my confinement? what prison and confinement?" Puzzled by the Alter Rebbe's response, the man stated, "but you were in a prison far away." The Alter Rebbe looked deeply into the man eyes and said, "When one's Soul is truly close to G-d, anyplace one is confined, no matter how small or seemingly bleak the space, that place is just a different abode for that Soul to speak with G-d, Whose boundaries are always far beyond any bars or walls that surround It. Dear friend, I was never trapped in a prison. I was just in place where I communicated with the Infinite in a different way."

Insight: A man can live in a castle and feel trapped, and a man can be in a prison and be free. It all depends upon how deep the inner faith in one's Soul to find the Infinite anywhere.

Question: Where in your life can you see deeper into the Divine?

Agreement: I, _____, agree and commit to, for myself, to seeing that my "right here, right now" contains much of what I need.

The Power Of Choice

The head Rabbi gave a teaching to a group of Rabbi's upon the verse of Torah, "Before you is the Blessing and the curse, choose wisely." One of the Rabbi's asked, "How can something be both a Blessing and a curse?" To illustrate the point, Rabbi, called each of the younger Rabbi's into his office, one at a time. On the head Rabbi's desk, was a flat metal object. As each Rabbi entered the office, the head Rabbi asked them the question, "What is the object upon my desk, and what is its purpose?" Each Rabbi, answered different. One Rabbi said, "A knife to eat with." Another Rabbi said, "A small pry bar to open something with." Another said, "A weapon to protect yourself with." After each of them had made their choice, the head Rabbi went back to classroom. The young Rabbi's then asked him, which one of them was correct about the metal object on his desk. The head Rabbi said, "Everyone and no one." One of the young Rabbis finally asked, "Then what is the flat metal object upon your desk? Is it a knife, or pry bar, or a weapon?" The Rabbi took a moment and then said, "Until I pick it up and I choose what purpose, good or bad, to use it for, it's just a flat piece of metal."

Insight: It is not the object, but our intention and the way we choose to use that which is around us, that denotes if things are blessings or curses.

Question: Where in your life can you use your power of choice to create blessings?

Agreement: I,_____, agree and commit to, for myself, to understanding that I have the power within to use choose and create the blessings.

Impossible Faith

One night, a Rabbi with a great vision for the world, heard a knock at his door. He answered it and before him was standing Fear. Immediately Fear said, "What are doing? The standard, the goal, the vision you have for the world is impossible. You have set the bar too high, you will never even touch it. It is impossible, I tell you, impossible." The Rabbi said, "Impossible is just a word, not a way. I only need a little faith and space in the impossible to succeed!" Then, fear asked, "How can one have faith and space in the impossible and succeed?" The Rabbi said, "I have faith in the impossible, by creating a space for the Light to enter. For a little light and space transforms the IMPOSSIBLE to I'M POSSIBLE because it IS possible!" With that, Fear disappeared, and standing in its place, was Courage.

Insight: To transform impossible to I'm possible requires only a space of belief.

Question: Where in your life can you transform a fear into faith?

Agreement: I, _____, agree and commit to, for myself, to confronting my fears by understanding they are transformable.

The Custodian & The Angels

Inspired By My Father & Mother
For Always Treating Everyone With High Respect

A man noticed at his temple, that the custodian always stayed an extra-long time. He could not lock the temple until the custodian finished cleaning. One day, he asked the custodian, "Why do you spend so long cleaning, and I notice you clean outside the temple as well, which is not your job?" The custodian said, "I am honored to clean the temple. I feel I am assisting G-d, for many bring their problems for G-d to solve and clean. I feel, I am close to G-d in cleaning up after His People as well." Suddenly, behind the custodian, the man saw the spirit of the Prophet Elijah, and host of other Angels, carrying the Prayers of the People up to Heaven for their lives to be helped and "cleaned". From that night on, the man assisted the custodian in cleaning up the temple.

Insight: Treat everyone as if they are already Divinely assisted, because when you get right down to it, they are.

Question: Where am I disrespecting others and how can I treat, myself and them, better by seeing them a little deeper and beyond society labels?

Agreement: I,_____ agree and commit to seeing the higher purpose in myself and others and understanding that all is not as it seems.

The True Success Of Failure

With great applause, a young Rabbi finished giving his first teaching at the local temple about achieving your dreams in life through true Emunah (Faith) and not fearing your own success. The head Rabbi came up to him and congratulated him upon his fine lessons to the community!!! The young Rabbi just stood there staring at the floor. The head Rabbi asked him, "What seems to be the matter? You've just accomplished something that will lead you to great successes!!!" The young Rabbi bitterly said, "There were a few people in attendance who were not really paying attention to me or my teaching. They must not want to succeed." "Fool," said the head Rabbi, "Why do you focus on the few who were not paying attention. Why do you not focus on those who were sitting on the edge of their seats, who cared enough to come, who were there eagerly listening to learn every word you were brave enough to say. Even those who YOU believe were not paying attention were still there to see and support you! I see you too are afraid of your own success."

Insight: Success is focused on our message and on those who are listening.

Question: Where in your life could you be more focused on your message, more then the approval of the crowd?

Agreement: I, _____, agree to and commit, for myself, to being focused on my purpose and message no matter what fears I may have.

The Ink Of The Story

One day, a man who felt his life was filled with stories of despair, asked a Rabbi, "If G-d is all powerful, why are people's lives filled with so many stories of despair?" The Rabbi replied, "To G-d, each person is a pen and they have the power of freewill to write their own stories from how they see their experiences. How each person chooses to write their story is up to them, not G-d alone." The man asked, "So, who would choose to write a story of despair?" The Rabbi said, "No one." The man then asked, "So why, as I asked, are people's stories filled with despair when G-d is all powerful?" Finally, the Rabbi said, "That is simple, it is not the pen, but the ink inside the pen that writes the story. If one fills their pen, their mind, soul and body, with the ink of regret, shame and doubt, the story cannot be written without the ink stains of despair. When one chooses to ink their stories with faith, their stories will reflect not despair, but the untapped power that always resides within the pen. The proof that G-d is all powerful is that He allows even a fool to be a fool until he learns to change, not the pen and his circumstance, but the ink inside."

Insight: All stories can be written from a weak or strong perspective depending on how strong WE CHOOSE to be.

Question: Where in your life could you rewrite your past stories into lessons of power?

Agreement: I,_____, commit and agree to, for myself, to writing my story (past, present and future) from a place of deeper faith and empowerment.

A Flood Of Tears

How Noah's Tears Start The Flood

There is a little known story about Noah's fourth son. It is written that when Noah was about to set sail with the Ark, he ran after his fourth son. This son was always rebellious and never believed in Noah. Yet, Noah still went after him to try again to talk him into boarding the Ark. Time was getting late and Noah was searching for his son in the hills when a Heavenly Voice said, "He is the son of your loins, not of your spirit." Noah looked a little more anyways, until he finally saw his fourth son who still choose to ignore all Noah's cries to him. A Heavenly Voice finally said, "He can't hear you, he never will." Noah began to weep and weep, and the rain began to fall like tears from Heaven as Noah returned to the Ark without him.

Insight: It is not always possible for others to see our mission, no matter how great it is.

Question: Where in your life are you trying to convince someone who may need to learn it on their own?

Agreement: I,_____, agree and commit, for myself, to following my path and mission despite those who will not be part of it.

The Beauty Of The King

One day, two men sought to see the King. For they heard the King was giving a great reward for those who could comprehend His Way. They both went to the Royal House, and inquired upon how to accomplish this. So, one of the King's Advisers, gave to each of them, the Book of the King, and Books for the rituals and customs they would need to learn, so that when they entered the King's Realm they would understand the King and His Ways. They were then told to return in a few months time. They thanked the King's adviser and then each went upon their way. Each studied very hard, but each had different motives for seeing the King. After a few months they returned. The first man understood most all of the books, the rituals and customs. The advisers who surrounded and guarded the King, saw this in the first man and he was escorted into the King's Private Realm. A moment later, the first man left weeping and heartbroken. The second man then went stood before the advisers and guards of the King. He did not grasp all the meanings, nor customs or rituals. Those around the King were suspicious of him and stopped him, but the Queen, on the other hand, saw into the man's heart and soul and approached with Her Radiance. Those who were blocking the man, bowed their heads, and step back from the Divine Presence & Power of the Queen, who personally escorted the man himself, into the Private Realms of the King, where the Three of them talked for many days. Upon leaving the Realm of the King, this second man was stopped by the first man. The first man asked him, "What secret did you possess that I did not? What magic were you able to gleam from the books that I did not?" The second man replied, "I do not know of any secret or magic. I only had my faith. I only know, I wanted to behold the Beauty of the King."

Insight: What we carry in our hearts and soul can be more powerful than the rituals and abstract understandings we have.

Question: Where in your life are you relying too much on intellect alone?

Agreement: I,_____, agree and commit to, for myself, to understanding the heart is as important as the mind.

ACKNOWLEDGEMENTS

I would like to thank my mother & father, William & Arlene Kingston, as well as my sister, Wendy & her husband Eric S. Mintz & my nieces Sabina & Juliet.

The Love Between You

Written For

My Father Mother,
William & Arlene Kingston

The Love Between You

One day,

Two soul-mates who had spent a whole lifetime together

Were going over the events of their lives.

As they looked over their many struggles and hardships,

They noticed that during their worst moments

It seemed that it was only each other

That pulled the other through,

It seemed that it was only their togetherness and faith

That held their lives together.

One day the L-rd appeared before them and they asked,

"L-rd, during our worst trials and tribulations

It seems it was only our togetherness

That held our lives together,

It seemed was only our togetherness

That kept our faith alive,

Where in all this was the Presence of G-d?"

The L-rd replied: "My precious children,

My beautiful Creations

I

Was the love between you"

ABOUT ERIC

Eric Sander Kingston is a master strategist, martial artist and composer. Best known for rapid transformational techniques, Eric uses a specifically created system of strategic drills, martial arts, original writings, to transfer specific techniques, and practical tools, to his clients. Eric's system empowers people to breakthrough their fear, and cultivate a deep, internal power of awareness, allowing them greater access to achieve their goals, and cultivate a life of stability and sustainable success.

Connect with Eric directly, for personal, or group, training, consultation, custom written works, or to have Eric personally transform your corporation or event, visit:

www.ericsanderkingston.com

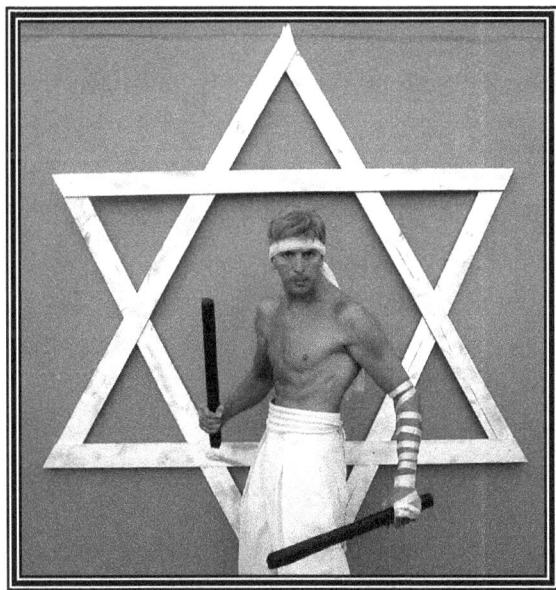

Wish On Wisdom Philosophy

Every race, religion and region has great wisdom to offer humanity. The Wish On Wisdom parables seek to impart this wisdom to create bridges of unity between all peoples of our planet earth.

www.wishonwisdom.com

*"The world is a narrow bridge,
the main thing is not to be afraid."*
Rabbi Nachman of Breslov

OTHER PUBLICATIONS
BY CHILD-TIME PUBLISHERS:
Established 1988

www.childtimepublishers.com

THE PRIMORDIAL WAY
Strategies To Inner Self Mastery
Written By Eric Sander Kingston

Eric Sander Kingston's newest book on internal strategy & philosophy of inner conflict to achieve non-duality and start transforming inner fears.

Please Note: This book is NOT intended for beginners who do not have some background in ancient energy literature, conflict resolution based on transformation towards inner mutual understanding or for Martial Artists who do not grasp Gandhi's Wisdom: *"The greatest demons in the world are those running around our own hearts."*

"It does not matter how many men you defeat! If you do not conquer your inner demons, you will pass your demons onto your child as your parent passed theirs onto you."

From the Film Dragon

The Primordial Way

Strategies To Inner Self Mastery

By Master Strategist
Eric Sander Kingston

AFRICAN WOMEN'S WISDOM
Original Parables
Based On The Proverbs Of Africa
To Empower The Feminine
Written By Eric Sander Kingston

Original one paragraph Parables with an interactive edge designed for personal power and transformation based upon the wisdom of African culture.

African Women's Wisdom

Original Parables
Based On The Proverbs Of Africa

By Eric Sander Kingston

THE HIDDEN DOOR
26 Original Rabbinic Parables
To Reveal The Concealed

26 Original Parables with an interactive edge designed for personal power and transformation.

The Bagels Are Coming!

A Humorous Look At How Bagels Bring Peace To The World.

Written and Illustrated by Arlene Kingston

Paperback,

Library Of Congress Number: 88-63105

ISBN: 0-929934-00-8
ISBN: 0-929934-00-8

A HUMOROUS LOOK AT HOW BAGELS BRING PEACE TO THE WORLD

THE BAGELS

ARE COMING!

by arlene Kingston

NOTES

www.ingramcontent.com/pod-product-compliance
Lightning Source LLC
Chambersburg PA
CBHW060624030426
42337CB00018B/3186